THE SUNDAY TIMES

Make Every Minute Count

THIRD EDITION

Marion E Haynes

KOGAN PAGE | CREATING SUCCESS

This edition published in 2009
Reprinted 2010

Kogan Page India Private Limited
4737/23 Ansari Road,
Daryaganj
New Delhi 110 002

ISBN: 978-81-7554-130-6

Published by Vinod Vasishtha for Kogan Page India Private Limited,
4737/23 Ansari Road, Daryaganj, New Delhi - 110 002.

Printed and bound at Raj Press, R-3, Inderpuri, New Delhi - 110 012.

contents

about this book

Make Every Minute Count is unlike most books. It has a unique self-paced format that encourages a reader to become personally involved. Designed to be 'read with a pencil', it offers an abundance of exercises, activities, assessments and cases that invite participation. Its objective is to help a person accomplish more in the time available.

Make Every Minute Count can be used effectively in a number of ways. Here are some possibilities:

- **Individual study.** Because the book is self-instructional, all that is needed is a quiet place, some time and a pencil. By completing the activities and exercises, a reader should receive not only valuable feedback, but also practical ideas about steps for self-improvement.
- **Workshops and seminars.** The book is ideal for assigned reading prior to a workshop or seminar. With the basics in hand, the quality of the participation should improve. More time can be spent on concept extensions and applications during the programme. The book can also be effective when a trainer distributes it at the beginning of a session and leads participants through the contents.

- **Distance learning.** Copies can be sent to those not able to attend head office training sessions.

One thing is for sure: even after it has been read, this book will serve as excellent reference material which can be easily reviewed.

preface

The first edition of this book enjoyed tremendous success. Over 100,000 copies of the US edition were sold and it was published in 12 other countries. This third edition has all the popular features of the original plus a section featuring time-saving electronic innovations and another offering time-saving tips for travellers.

Make Every Minute Count can help you to become a better manager of time; however, it won't manage time for you. That is your responsibility. Effective time management is an experience in self-discipline, and you are the key to success. If you make use of the principles and techniques in this book, you will manage your time with less stress and accomplish more.

The objectives of this book are to:

- help you assess how you use time now;
- make you aware of that portion of time over which you have control;
- teach you how to make the most effective use of the time you control;
- help you to handle time not under your control in a more efficient way;
- allow you to use time the way you choose (work, play or rest).

Better time management is within your grasp. If you are motivated to complete this book and apply the ideas it contains, you will gain from the experience. I hope you will.

Marion E Haynes

1

the basics of time management

Time is a unique resource. Day to day, everyone has the same amount. It cannot be accumulated. You can't turn it on or off. It can't be replaced. It has to be spent at the rate of 60 seconds every minutes.

Time management, like other management, benefits from analysis and planning. To understand and apply time management principles, you must know not only how to use time, but also what problems you encounter in using it, and what causes them. From this base you can learn to improve your effectiveness and efficiency through better time management.

Time management is a personal process and must fit your style and circumstances. It takes a strong commitment to change old habits; however, this choice is available and yours for the taking. If you choose to apply the principles in this book, you will obtain the rewards that come from better time investment.

> The questionnaire on the next page will assist you in looking at your current time management attitudes and practices. It will help you to identify the things you will want to concentrate on as you complete this book.

we all get 168 hours per week, how do you use yours?

Tick the column that best describes how you feel or act. Then review your responses and focus on each item to see if it represents an opportunity to improve your management of time.

	Usually	Sometimes	Rarely
1. Do you normally spend time the way you really want to?	______	______	______
2. Do you often feel harried, and obliged to do things you really don't want to do?	______	______	______
3. Do you feel a sense of accomplishment from your work?	______	______	______
4. Do you work longer hours than your colleagues?	______	______	______
5. Do you regularly take work home at evenings or weekends?	______	______	______
6. Do you feel stress because of too much work?	______	______	______
7. Do you feel guilty about not doing a better job?	______	______	______
8. Do you consider your job to be fun?	______	______	______
9. Can you find blocks of uninterrupted time when you need to?	______	______	______
10. Do you feel in control of the way you use your time?	______	______	______
11. Do you maintain a regular exercise programme?	______	______	______

12. Do you take holidays or long weekends as often as you would like?	_____	_____	_____
13. Do you put off doing the difficult, boring or unpleasant parts of your job?	_____	_____	_____
14. Do you feel you must always be busy doing something productive?	_____	_____	_____
15. Do you feel guilty when you occasionally leave early?	_____	_____	_____

Adapted from *Successful Time Management*, by Jack D Ferner, pp 6–7, New York, NY: John Wiley & Sons, © 1980, by permission of the publisher.

2

what controls your time?

The best starting place to improve you use of time is to determine the extent to which you control the time available to you. No one has total control over a daily schedule. Someone or something will always make demands. However, everyone has *some* control, and probably more than they realise.

Some time ('working hours' or 'school hours') is regulated and should be used for those activities. Even within this structured time, there are opportunities to select which tasks or activities to handle and what priority to assign to that task. It is the exercise of these discretionary choices that allows you to control your time.

control of your time

As an employee, your scheduled work hours should be used in pursuit of company objectives. In school or college, your time should be spent studying and learning. To this extent, the use of your time is often controlled by specific tasks or assignments. However, several degrees of freedom usually exist in any specific time period. Where are you? (Circle one of the numbers below.)

I have total control	10 9 8 7 6 5 4 3 2 1 0	I have no control

Tasks or activities that allow me personal control of my time	**Tasks or activities that limit my control of my time**
______________________	______________________
______________________	______________________
______________________	______________________
______________________	______________________
______________________	______________________
______________________	______________________
______________________	______________________
______________________	______________________
______________________	______________________
______________________	______________________

3

three tests of time

Although the examples described in this book are basically from the business world, similar principles apply to other aspects of your life.

Analysing how you use your time at present is the first step to achieving better control of it. You must have specific, reliable information before you can identify opportunities for improvement. The best way to gather information is to keep a time log.

Once this information has been recorded, you should examine it from three points of view – necessity, appropriateness and efficiency. This should allow you to discontinue certain tasks, delegate others and/or find ways to increase efficiency through technology, new procedures or personal work habits.

A careful analysis can often earn you another eight to ten hours each week to spend on activities of your choice.

1. the test of necessity

First you should scrutinise each activity to be sure it is necessary – not just nice, but necessary. It is common to do things when their usefulness is past, ie monthly reports where the information is no longer used. This 'test of necessity' should help to reduce your tasks to the essential elements.

2. the test of appropriateness

Once the essential tasks have been identified, the next step should determine who should perform them, ie appropriateness in terms of department and/or skill level. There are probably activities that could be given to others. You may also find you are doing work beneath your skill level which can easily be reassigned.

3. the test of efficiency

The third analysis examines tasks that remain. Once satisfied you are doing necessary work you should then ask: 'Is there a better way?' This will encourage you to find a faster way, using better technology, or establish better procedures to handle recurring activities.

analyse for effective time utilisation

In your own words, and from your own situation, list opportunities for more effective use of your time using the three tests described above.

the test of necessity

These are opportunities to eliminate some unnecessary tasks or activities:

____

____

____

____

the test of appropriateness

These are opportunities to make better use of time by reassigning tasks or activities to others:

____

____

____

____

the test of efficiency

These are opportunities to become more efficient by using technology or developing better procedures:

____

____

____

____

There are only three ways to make better use of your time:

1. Discontinue low-priority tasks or activities.
2. Find someone else to take some of your work.
3. Be more efficient at what you do.

4

benefits of better time utilisation

When you are able to make better use of time, you can benefit from completion of longer-term activities such as:

- *Career planning.* Set a course for your future and lay out a plan to achieve it. Move to a proactive mode. Take charge of your own destiny.
- *Reading.* Keeping up to date is increasingly important in today's complex world. More time will allow you to read job-related materials, study new subjects, or lean more about a hobby or activity.
- *Communicating.* Extra time will allow you to improve and/or initiate interpersonal relationships.
- *Relaxing.* You need to plan time for relaxation. When you do not take time off from the daily grind your health may suffer, or you may 'burn out'.
- *Thinking.* Improved methods and new opportunities come about as a result of innovation. More time will allow you to develop strategies and think through plans to establish and achieve significant new challenges.

case study 4.1
Sheila learns through experience

Three months ago Sheila looked forward to her promotion to supervisor. After four years in the department she was confident of her abilities, and knew her staff were capable and experienced.

Today, Sheila isn't so sure she was cut out to be a supervisor. There seems to be no end to her working day. During office hours her day is filled, assigning work and reviewing results. Also there is a steady flow of visitors, and the phone rings constantly. In the evening, when she would like to relax, she has to take care of administrative matters such as reading mail, answering letters, preparing budgets and completing performance appraisals.

In frustration, Sheila asked her friend Carol to join her for lunch. Sheila said she had something important to talk about. At lunch, she told Carol she was thinking about giving up her supervisor's job. She said she just couldn't face a career of working 60 hours a week. Carol listened and then said there might be another way. If the only issue was the time required to do the job, perhaps a review of how Sheila was using her time might help. After listening to Sheila describe a typical week, Carol asked the following questions:

- Since she described her staff as 'capable and experienced', why was Sheila spending so much time assigning work and checking results?
- Who were the drop-in visitors? Could some be screened out?
- Could the departmental secretary take phone calls and refer some to others or have non-urgent calls returned at a more convenient time?
- Could some of Sheila's work be done by someone else?

With those thoughts in mind, Sheila returned to her office with a commitment to take a closer look at her use of time.

Consider Sheila's situation and answer the following questions:

1. Does she appear to be making effective use of delegation? ________________________________

   ____

2. If her visitors are employees, how might she avoid interruptions? __________________________

   ____

3. Should Sheila consider establishing a 'quiet time' when she would receive no calls or visitors? If so, when might be the best time of day? __________________

   ____

4. Sheila feels she should assign all departmental work and check all results. Is there a more efficient way?

   ____

   ____

5. What other ways could Sheila gain control over her use of time? ______________________________

   ____

   ____

how would you handle these situations?

Listed below are situations where an opportunity exists to improve the use of time. Read each example and then check the choice you feel is the best response.

1. As Jean checks time cards each week, she spends two hours summarising the hours of employees who have been away because of sickness or holiday. She is aware that the wages department gathers this same information and provides it to all department heads. What should she do?
   - ☐ Continue summarising the information.
   - ☐ Stop summarising the information.
   - ☐ Point out the duplication to her supervisor and request permission to stop doing the work.
2. John likes to interview job candidates. He is excellent at matching candidates with job openings. Now that John is manager, he still spends about five hours a week interviewing even though he has staff to handle this. As a result, he often takes work home. What should John do?
   - ☐ Say with his present practice. He's the manager and has the right to do as he wishes.
   - ☐ Delegate some of the administrative work to one of his staff so he can keep interviewing.
   - ☐ Stop interviewing except when the workload exceeds his staff's capacity.
3. When Gloria assumed her present job she noticed the quality of expense summaries she received from accounting was inadequate. Expenses were incorrectly allocated and often two months passed before accounts were correct. In order to have up-to-date, accurate information, Gloria now spends six hours a week keeping her own records. What should she do?
   - ☐ Continue to keep her own records. It is the only way to know they will be done correctly.
   - ☐ Stop keeping her own records and use what the accounts department furnishes.
   - ☐ Discuss with the accounts department a way to get the information she needs.

4. George is an assistant in the personnel department. Several times each month employees ask George to work out an estimate of their retirement benefits. He does each estimate by hand. Each estimate takes 45 minutes. What should George do?
   - ☐ Continue his present practice. It seems to work all right.
   - ☐ Refuse to prepare estimates except for employees planning to retire within one year.
   - ☐ Develop and produce a computer-generated summary sheet which can be personalised.
5. Carlos distributes a computer-generated report to field offices quarterly. A couple of his field colleagues have told him that they don't use the report. What should he do?
   - ☐ Ignore the comments and continue to distribute the report.
   - ☐ Stop distributing the report and see what happens.
   - ☐ Survey all field offices and recommend a change in the report based on what is found.
6. Janice receives 25 to 40 enquiries daily from members about the association's medical insurance coverage. Each one receives a personal reply. This part of her job consumes most of her time, leaving little time for her other duties. What should she do?
   - ☐ Continue providing personal service to members – they are entitled to it.
   - ☐ Develop a form letter and post it along with a plan summary in response to all enquiries.
   - ☐ Study recent enquiries to see what questions are most frequently asked and develop a series of replies on the word processor that can be personalised.

The author feels the third choice is best in all situations.

5

prime time

When considering a daily schedule, it's a good idea to keep your energy cycle in mind. Some people are at their best early in the morning.. Others peak in the afternoon. Whenever possible, try to plan your daily schedule to match your 'prime time'. You will now always have control but consider such ideas as reading, responding to mail or returning phone calls after lunch if your 'prime time' is in the morning.

On the facing page is an exercise to help you visualise your energy cycle.

Typical energy cycle

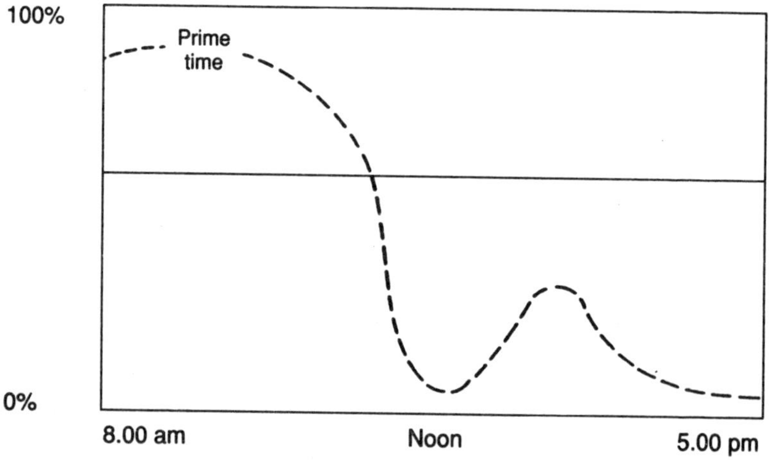

chart your energy cycle

Fill in the beginning and ending time of your day on the following diagram. Then draw a line through the day reflecting your typical energy cycle.

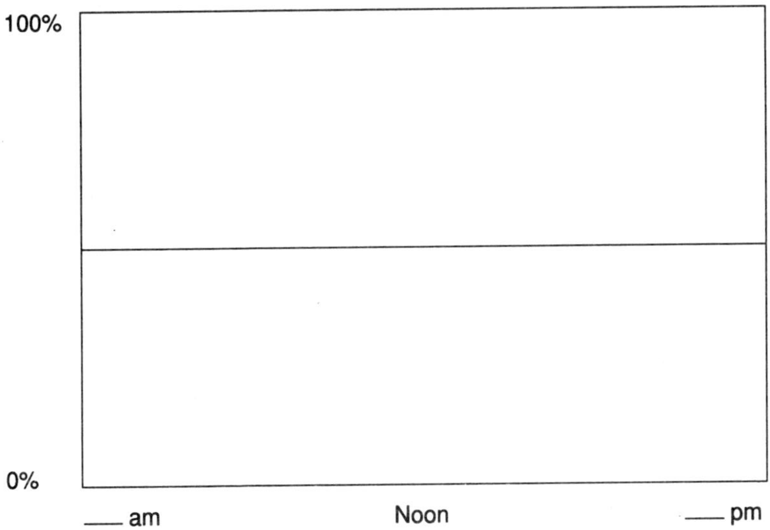

1. Do you arrange your working day to take advantage of your energy cycle? ______________________
2. What could you do differently to make better use of your period of peak energy? ______________________

   ____

   ____

   ____

6

setting priorities

When opportunities exceed resources, decisions must be made. Nowhere is this more apparent than in the use of time. Since time cannot be manufactured, you must decide what to do and what not to do.

Setting priorities in the use of time is a two-step process: (1) listing things that need to be done, and (2) prioritising items on the list. (See facing page.)

Use the ABC method to determine your priorities by planning each item on your list into one of the following categories:

- Priority A – 'Must do'. These are the critical items. Some may fall into this category because of management directives, important customer requirements, significant deadlines, or opportunities for success or advancement.
- Priority B – 'Should do'. These are items of medium value. Items in this category may contribute to improved performance but are not essential or do not have critical deadlines.
- Priority C – 'Nice to do'. This is the lowest value category. While interesting or fun, they could be eliminated, postponed, or scheduled for slack periods.

Your As, Bs and Cs are flexible, depending on the date your list is prepared. Priorities change over time. Today's 'B' may become tomorrow's 'A' as an important deadline approaches. Likewise, today's 'A' may become tomorrow's 'C', if it did not get accomplished in time and/or circumstances change.

Obviously, it is not worth while to spend much time on a task of modest value. On the other hand, a project of high value is worth the time invested. Only good planning will allow you to reap the benefits of time wisely invested.

Use the form below to practise setting priorities.

My priorities for the week of: ______________

Priority A – Must do

____

____

____

____

____

____

Priority B – Should do

____

____

____

____

____

____

Priority C – Nice to do

____

____

____

____

____

____

criteria for setting priorities

judgement

You are the best judge of what you have to do. Let the pang of guilt you feel from not getting something done sharpen your judgement.

relativity

As you compare tasks or activities it should become clear that some are higher priority than others. You should always be guided by the question: 'What is the best use of my time right now?'

timing

Deadlines have a way of dictating priorities. Also important, but often overlooked, is a required starting time in order to finish a project by the deadline.

two hours a day

If you had two extra hours each day, how would you use them? Answer by putting an X in front of each statement that applies. Add your own ideas.

With two extra hours each day I would:

____ 1. Do more planning.
____ 2. Do more reading.
____ 3. Spend more time on new work projects.
____ 4. Spend more time with my family/friends.
____ 5. Begin or expand an exercise programme.
____ 6. Spend more time on personal financial matters.
____ 7. Start or expand a hobby.
____ 8. (Add your own)
____ 9. ______________________________
____ 10. ______________________________
____ 11. ______________________________
____ 12. ______________________________

review worksheet

1. The following are ways in which I could make better use of my time:
   - ______________________________
   - ______________________________
   - ______________________________
   - ______________________________

2. The major roadblocks to a more effective and efficient use of my time are:
   - ________________
   - ________________
   - ________________
   - ________________

3. If I 'found' five hours a week, I would use that time to:
   - ________________
   - ________________
   - ________________
   - ________________

4. The following activities involve a lot of my time, yet don't seem to contribute much to my objectives:
   - ________________
   - ________________
   - ________________
   - ________________

how to control your use of time

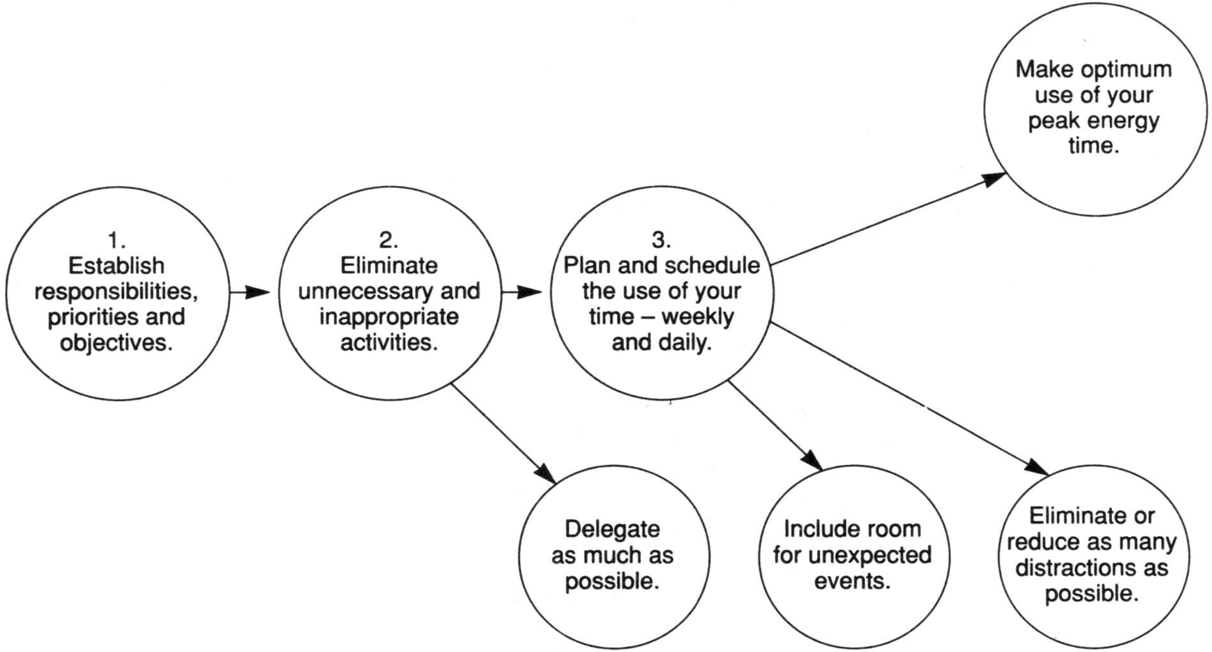

self-assessment questionnaire

The following statements summarize the principles presented in Chapters 1 to 6. Tick those that apply to you. Review items you do not tick to see if an opportunity may exist for future efficiency.

- ☐ I know when my peak energy period occurs.
- ☐ I have adjusted my daily routine to make maximum use of my peak energy.
- ☐ I have a written summary of my responsibilities.
- ☐ I have listed my objectives for the next quarter.
- ☐ I have prioritised my use of time.
- ☐ I have eliminated all unnecessary and inappropriate tasks.
- ☐ I have studied ways to improve efficiency in handling routine matters.
- ☐ I delegate whenever logical and possible.
- ☐ I plan what I want to accomplish each week.
- ☐ I prepare a daily 'things to do' list.
- ☐ I leave some time for the unexpected each day.
- ☐ I realise that I can't do everything and must choose the best alternatives.

7

time-management planning

Planning is a complex process. Some people are good at it, others aren't. Some seem so caught up in activities and deadlines that they claim there is no time to plan. Yet planning is the key to relieve the stress of too little time. It is the way to structure your future.

Planning makes two contributions that bring order to your life. First, it tells you how to get from where you are to where you want to be. Second, it identifies the resources required to get you there. Through planning, you know when to begin something to complete it on schedule, and what it is going to cost.

Planning is either long term or short term. In this book, long-term plans describe what you expect to accomplish during the next three months as well as any project whose duration exceeds a week. Short-term plans cover what you expect to accomplish today or this week, although these may be steps towards longer-term objectives.

my time frame

long-term objectives

These are my objectives for the next quarter, plus my projects that will take longer than a week to complete:

____

____

____

____

____

____

short-term goals

These are the things that need doing this week (including steps towards longer-term objectives):

____

____

____

____

____

____

8

long-term planning aids

Planning aids are a critical part of effective time management. It simply is not possible to remember everything. Three common planning aids are presented on the following pages. These are an *action-planning worksheet*, a *milestone chart* and a *PERT diagram*. From these alternatives you can select the technique that best fits the type of work you do. Using a planning aid will help to bring order to your life.

One word of caution – don't get too elaborate. Don't spend more time drawing and updating planning aids than is required. In other words, your planning should save you time, not cost you time.

Regardless of the technique you choose, your master calendar should record all activities. Note the due dates for each action step, as well as the project completion date. When others are responsible for a step in your plan, ensure you have assigned a follow-up date. Also, always know who is responsible for each step – and the date by when their action is to be completed.

The long-term planning aids available are:

- action-planning worksheet;
- milestone chart;
- PERT diagram.

action-planning worksheet

Action-planning worksheets can vary greatly in their complexity. The simplest ones show only those steps required to complete a project. Additional information (such as beginning dates, targeted completion dates, cost estimates and who is responsible) can be added to the basic worksheet.

example

Action-planning worksheet

Objective: *Publish a work planning and review workbook by 31 May.*

Action step	Estimated time	Target	Assigned responsibility
1. Write draft	15 days	April 15	Self
2. Type draft	10 days	April 25	Secretary
3. Proof-read	5 days	April 30	Self & secretary
4. Draw cover	5 days	April 20	Graphics
5. Type final	10 days	May 10	Key entry
6. Proof-read	3 days	May 13	Self & secretary
7. Make corrections	2 days	May 15	Key entry
8. Draw figures	5 days	May 15	Graphics
9. Reproduce	15 days	May 30	Print shop
10. Deliver books		May 31	Print shop

Action-planning worksheet

Objective: ______________________________

____

____

____

Action step	Target date	Cost		Assigned responsibility
		£	Time	

milestone chart

A milestone chart displays graphically the relationship between the steps in a project. To create one, list the steps required to finish the project and estimate the time required for each step. Then lists the steps down the left side of the chart, with dates shown along the bottom. Draw a line across the chart for each step, starting at the planned beginning date and ending on the completion date of that step. Once completed, you should be able to see the flow of the action steps and their sequence (including those that can be underway at the same time).

The usefulness of a milestone chart will be improved by also charting actual progress. This is usually done by drawing a line in a different colour under the original line to show actual beginning and completion dates of each step.

example

Objective: *Publish a work planning and review workbook by 31 May.*

Action steps with time estimates:

1. Write draft	15 days	6. Proof-read	3 days
2. Type draft	10 days	7. Make corrections	2 days
3. Proof-read	5 days	8. Draw figures	5 days
4. Draw cover	5 days	9. Reproduce	15 days
5. Type final	10 days	10. Deliver books	

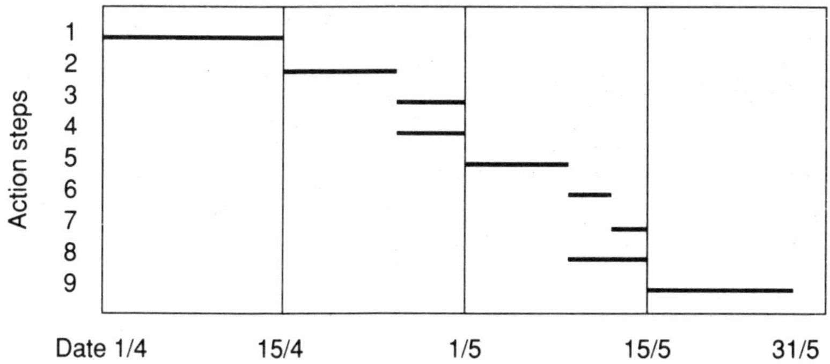

practise a milestone chart

Select a project and practise drawing a milestone chart.

Objective: ______________________________

____

____

Action steps with time estimates:

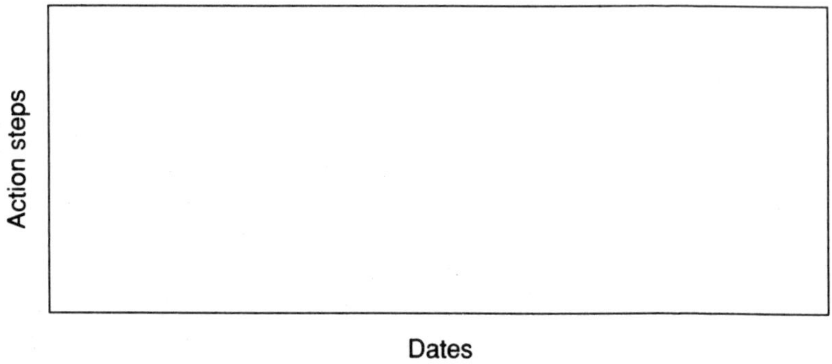

PERT diagram

PERT stands for Programme Evaluation and Review Technique. It is a diagram that represents an added degree of sophistication in the planning process. To draw one, list the steps required to finish a project and estimate the time required to complete each step. Then draw a network of relationships among the steps. The number of the step is shown in a circle and the time to complete the step is shown on the line leading to the next circle. Steps that must be completed first are shown in order to clarify proper sequencing. Steps that can be underway at the same time are shown on different paths.

A PERT diagram not only shows the relationship between various steps in a project, it also serves as an easy way to calculate the 'critical path'. The critical path is shown as a broken line in the example opposite. It identifies essential steps that must be completed on time in order not to delay completion of the total project.

example

Objective: *Publish a work planning and review workbook by 31 May.*

Action steps with time estimates:

Step	Time	Step	Time
1. Write draft	15 days	6. Proof-read	3 days
2. Type draft	10 days	7. Make corrections	2 days
3. Proof-read	5 days	8. Draw figures	5 days
4. Draw cover	5 days	9. Reproduce	15 days
5. Type final	10 days	10. Deliver books	

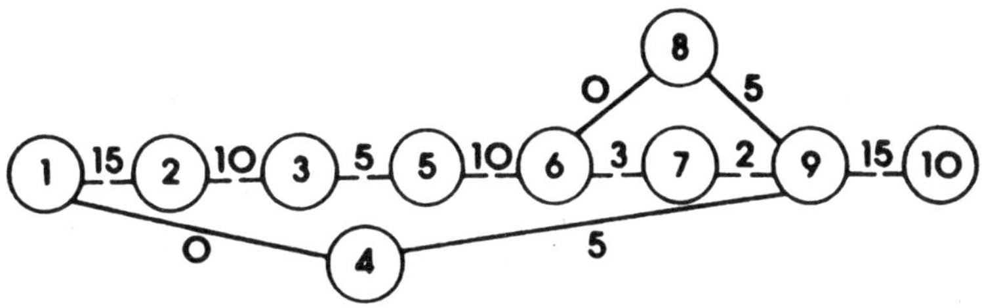

The usefulness of the PERT diagram can be increased by colouring each step as it is completed. Actual time may be written over the estimated time to maintain a running tally of actual versus planned time along the critical path.

practise drawing a PERT diagram

Select a project and use it to practise drawing a PERT diagram.

Objective: ______________________________

____

____

Action steps with time estimates:

______	______	______	______
______	______	______	______
______	______	______	______
______	______	______	______
______	______	______	______
______	______	______	______

9

short-term planning aids

Action steps in long-term plans must be listed in order of importance and integrated with your other demands. These discrete steps become part of your short-term plans. Short-term plans are best developed and scheduled on both a weekly and a daily basis.

weekly plans

A weekly plan should describe what you want to accomplish by the end of the week, and the activities required to get you there. Weekly plans can be developed on Friday for the following week, over the weekend, or on Monday morning. (Many people use commuting time for this activity.)

Weekly worksheets may be simple or complex. The example on the next page can serve as a starting point for your short-term plans.

Once completed, your worksheet should be kept handy for frequent reference. Daily activities should be transferred to a daily diary, and take place according to an assigned priority.

Weekly planning worksheet

For week of: ____________

Objectives:

1. ____________
2. ____________
3. ____________

Activities	A/B/C priority	Estimated time	Assigned day

daily plans

The culmination of the planning process is the best use of your time each day. If you make a habit of a daily diary, many of your activities will already be recorded. This is the best starting place to develop your list of 'things to do today'.

A daily prioritised list is the best way to focus attention on your most important objectives. Work from the top of your list. If unexpected demands come up, assess their priority and handle them accordingly. Don't use something unexpected as an excuse for distraction. At the end of each day review what was accomplished and carry forward any items on your list that need completing. Integrate these with tomorrow's new items.

The format for your list is not important. It can be written anywhere in a diary on a plain sheet of paper or on a form that you develop yourself. Many stationers have a variety of planning forms available. The example below illustrates how simple a daily form can be. The example of the daily planning worksheet is more elaborate.

Use your 'things to do' list to lay out a daily schedule. It should reflect meetings and appointments, plus time to accomplish other priority items on your list.

Things to do today
Make travel arrangements
Attend budget review at 10.00 am
Complete salary proposals
Reserve conference room for Wednesday
Phone insurance agent
Make dentist appointment

daily planning worksheet

Things to do today

Date: ____________

Tasks to complete	**Done**	**Appointments to keep**
		7.00
		8.00
		9.00
		10.00
		11.00
		12.00
Phone calls to make	**Done**	
		1.00
		2.00
		3.00
People to see	**Done**	4.00
		5.00
		6.00
		7.00

10

conference planner

Do you need to communicate frequently with co-workers for information to complete your work? Often this causes an interruption they may find distracting. One way to handle the situation efficiently is to use a *conference planner.* (See the example on the following page.)

First enter the names of those you frequently call on. Then, as you think of an item you need to discuss, note it under the person's name. When it is time to have a conference, prioritise the list. Cross out unimportant items or those that can be handled better in some other way.

Conference planner		
Name:	Name:	Name:
Name:	Name:	Name:
Name:	Name:	Name:

11

characteristics of good planners

The following statements describe how people view different aspects of planning. Tick those statements that, in your opinion, reflect the views of a good planner.

- ☐ It is necessary to identify and operate within two time horizons. Anticipating events allow things to get done in the short term which contribute to achieving long-term objectives.
- ☐ An up-to-date master diary can be your most helpful planning tool. However, detailed project plans must be developed before valid entries can be made in it.
- ☐ When things begin to get hectic, a 'things to do today' list helps to focus attention on the highest priority items.
- ☐ Action planning worksheets, milestone charts and PERT diagrams are excellent planning aids when properly used.
- ☐ Planning contact with colleagues and staff will help to minimise the disruption of their schedules. One way to do this is to use a conference planner worksheet.

- The most effective approaches to planning are those tailored to meet individual needs. Concepts, procedures and worksheets are all subject to modification to fit individual circumstances.

---

case study 11.1
another day at the office

It was 7:20 am when Michael arrived at the office. He was early because he wanted to clear the backlog of work that had been piling up on his desk. He turned on the lights and started to go through yesterday's post. As he read the first piece, he realised he couldn't deal with it until a colleague arrived. He set it aside and went to the next. This item had potential application to a project he was working on, so he walked down the hall and made a copy for his personal use.

As he continued reading his post he came across a journal article of particular interest and became engrossed in it. He was startled to find as he looked up that others were arriving and it was nearly 9.00 o'clock.

He quickly pushed the remaining post to a corner of his desk and reached for a project file due tomorrow with at least two days' work yet to be completed. As he opened the file, Bill and Claire stopped by and invited him to join them for coffee. Michael decided he could spare 10 minutes. Bill and Claire were both anxious to share the details of a play they attended last night. Before Michael realised it, 30 minutes had passed and he hurried back to his office.

As Michael entered his office, the phone rang. It was Mr Wilson, his manager. There was a meeting schedule at 10:00. Could Michael sit in for him? There was something to be discussed that the department should know about. Michael looked at his watch. There wasn't enough time to get started on the project so he pushed the file aside and vowed to start on it immediately after lunch.

The afternoon wasn't any better. A few visitors, a few phone calls, a couple of letters and the day was over. Nothing had been accomplished on the project that was due tomorrow. As he stuffed papers into his briefcase, he wondered how Bill and Claire were able to attend plays during the evening.

Examine Michael's use of time:

1. Did he make good use of prime time? ______
2. Was he working on his highest priority task? ______
3. Did he seem able to say 'no'? ______
4. Did he practise task completion? ______
5. Does he seem to understand his problem? ______

12

common time-wasters

Everyone wastes time. It's a universal human failing. Some wasted time can be constructive because it helps you to relax or otherwise reduce tension. Other wasted time, however, can be frustrating. This is especially true when time is wasted because you are doing something less important or less fun than you might otherwise be doing.

The key question is, what else might you be doing that is of a higher personal priority? Taking a break, communicating with associates, talking on the telephone and reading are not time-wasters unless they keep you from your primary objectives.

Time-wasters usually arise from two sources. One is environment and the other is self. Some typical examples of each are shown on the facing page.

The next few pages will concentrate on ways for you to recognise and manage your most frequent time-wasters.

examples of common time-wasters

Self-generated		Environmental	
	See page		*See page*
Disorganisation	44	Visitors	48
Procrastination	45	Telephone calls	49
Inability to say 'No'	47	Junk mail	49
		Waiting for someone	50
		Unproductive meetings	50
		Crises	51
Others:		*Others:*	
Gossip		Coffee time conversations	
Unnecessary perfectionism		Unused reports	

13

self-generated time-wasters

disorganisation

Disorganisation is a key culprit for wasted time. Evidence of disorganisation shows up in the layout of a work area. If time is spent searching for misplaced items or wasted due to distractions which cause you to start and stop several times before a task is completed, then you need to evaluate your work area. Check it out. Is it efficient? Is it organised to minimise effort? Is there a free flow of materials and movement? Have you considered the placement of equipment such as the telephone and the calculator, the proximity of supplies that are frequently used, and your accessibility to active files?

Next, focus on your desk. Is your work area cluttered? How much time do you waste looking for things you know are there but can't find? When was the last time you used some of the items in and on your desk? Perhaps a clean-up is in order.

The old axiom, 'A place for everything and everything in its place' is the best advice for organising the information you need. Files should be set up for work in progress and kept handy. Everything relating to a particular project should be kept in one file folder. Files should be indexed for quick reference. Call-up procedures are required for items that need future action. A folder for current items received by mail, telephone or visit should be maintained and checked daily to see what needs to be done.

Finally, organise your approach to work. Practise completing your tasks. If interrupted, do not immediately jump to a new task. First, assess the priority of a request, and avoid getting involved in any new activity until it becomes your top priority. If an interruption comes by phone or personal visit, simply return to the task you were working on as soon as the interruption ends.

A plan for setting up a personal filing system is given on the following page.

procrastination

We all put things off. Typically, these items include boring, difficult, unpleasant, or onerous tasks that ultimately need completing. When this happens to you, consider the following ideas:

- Set a deadline to complete the task and stick with it.
- Build in a reward system. For example, tell yourself: 'When I finish that task I'm going to enjoy a nice meal' or 'I won't go home until I finish this task'.
- Arrange with someone (a colleague, secretary, etc) always to follow up with your progress on tasks you tend to put off.
- Do undesirable tasks early in the day so you can be finished with them.

dealing with procrastination

- Set a deadline
- Set up a reward system
- Arrange for follow-up
- Do it first
- Break job into small pieces
- Do it now!

how to set up a personal filing system

- It is not necessary to be too logical. It is your system, and no one else will be using it, so it only needs to make sense to you.
- Use a limited number of categories. For example, you may find the following five adequate:
  - *Projects.* In this category are individual files with information related to different projects you are working on.
  - *Instant tasks.* This category should have folders on little jobs to fill in your time when you have a few minutes. Perhaps low-priority letters to be answered, or general-interest articles to be read.
  - *Self-development.* This category contains folders related to training: books, articles, etc.
  - *Ideas.* This category contains items you wish to investigate further to improve your operation.
  - *Background information.* This category is a resource for various things you are involved with. Keep separate folders by topic and refer to them when you need statistics, examples, quotations, etc.
- It may be a good idea to colour code by priority within each category to draw attention to your most important items. This is easily accomplished by using colour highlighters and marking individual folders.

- Keep your filing up to date so time won't be wasted searching for an item.
- Review the contents of your files periodically to keep the volume of material to an essential minimum. This also will reduce time going through files when you are looking for something.

inability to say 'No'

At some point we all have demands on our time which exceed our ability to accommodate them. Here is where learning to say 'No' will come to the rescue. When you take on more than you can handle, the quality of your work will suffer and you would be better off taking on only what you can handle comfortably.

Saying 'No' doesn't need to offend. One approach is to offer an alternative. Rather than saying 'Yes' too often, try some of the following responses:

- 'I can take care of that but what I'm doing now will be delayed. Is your request more important?'
- 'I'll be glad to handle that for you. However, I can't get round to it until I finish what I'm doing. That will be...'
- I'm sorry I don't have time to take on any new work. I'll phone you when I have some spare time.'
- 'I appreciate your expression of confidence but I just can't fit it into my schedule right now. Sorry.'
- I'm sorry, I just can't do it. Have you considered asking...?'

environmental time-wasters

Even when you are well organised and making effective use of time, there will always be interruptions and distractions from outside sources. Here are ideas for handling some of the most common ones.

visitors

Controlling time taken up by visitors requires both courtesy and judgement. As a starting point, limit the number of people you invite to your work area. If you need to meet a colleague, go to his or her work area. This way you can simply excuse yourself once your purpose is accomplished. It is often more difficult to get people to leave your area than it is for you to leave theirs.

Discourage drop-in visitors by turning your desk away from the door. When people see you are busy, they tend not to interrupt. Also, you might consider closing your door (if you have one) when you need to concentrate.

When someone unexpectedly drops in, stand up to talk.

Don't invite your visitor to be seated unless you have the time. Usually, when you stand, your visitor will also stand. This should shorten the visit. If this does not work, be honest and say something like 'Thanks for dropping in. You'll have to excuse me now because I need to get this project finished.'

telephone calls

For many, telephones are a constant interruption. You can't eliminate all of them. You can, however, limit the amount of time they take. If you are fortunate enough to have someone to answer your phone, calls should be filtered. Review which calls need a personal follow-up, and delegate the others. Messages should be taken during periods when you do not wish to be interrupted.

When talking on the phone, limit social conversation. Provide short answers to questions. End the conversation when it has achieved its business purpose in a polite way.

post

A third distraction is your post. Unsolicited post arrives in an unending flood. If someone else sorts your post, give some guidelines on what you want to see (separated in two piles, 'information only' and 'action'), what should be routed to others, and what should be thrown out.

Learn to handle each item of post once. As you read it decide what action is required, and then take that action (even if it is only to put it into an action file). 'Information only' post can be saved and read at a more convenient time (ie commuting, waiting for appointments, over lunch, in the evening, etc).

You can save time by responding to some post by phone. If information is needed, it might be possible to have someone else phone and pass on what is required.

Another idea is to write a brief response in longhand on the original letter and post it back. If a record is needed, photocopy it before it is sent off.

waiting for someone

We all spend too much time waiting – for appointments, for meetings to begin, for others to complete something, for transport, and as we commute. Opportunities exist to make better use of this 'waiting' time.

Waiting need not be wasted time. Two approaches will help. First, don't spend unreasonable time waiting for others with whom you have appointments. If you go to someone's office and are not received promptly, leave word with a secretary to call you when the meeting is ready to start and return to your office.

The other way to make use of waiting time is to employ it productively. For example, read your post (including trade and professional journals), carry a notepad and pencil to develop plans or write letters, and/or carry a file of low priority items to complete.

A compact cassette recorder can help to improve your productivity during travel and commuting. Either listen to information tapes, or use the machine to record ideas and instructions for when you return to your office.

unproductive meetings

Time wasted in meetings comes from two sources – the meetings you call, and the meetings you attend.

When you call a meeting, plan what you want to accomplish. Keep attendees to a minimum number of appropriate people. Briefly explain your agenda and move directly to the purpose of the meeting. Establish a time limit. Keep the discussion on track by periodically summarising where you are. When the business has been completed, assign responsibilities, and establish follow-up dates to convert decisions to action, then adjourn the meeting.

A common time waster is the 'regular staff meeting'. Two suggestions can make significant improvements. First, set an agenda by asking 'What do we have to talk about today?' If more material is generated than can be handled in the available time, prioritise the list. If nothing significant is offered, adjourn the meeting. A second suggestion is to eliminate any discussion that involves only two participants. These should be handled as one-to-one sessions.

Before you attend someone else's meeting, make sure it is necessary for you to be there. If it is, arrive on time and be prepared to participate in the discussion. Avoid taking the discussion off track and/or prolonging it. Work to make the meeting productive. Add any follow-up items to your list of things to do within appropriate priority designation.

crises

Many people believe crises are unavoidable. That's only partly true. Unexpected events do occur which must be handled then and there. Many crises, however, are recurring events brought on by something that either was or was not done. When you delay something that needs doing, you are helping to create a future crises.

A starting point to reduce future crises is to review past crises. Are there patterns? You can often develop a response to recurring problems. For example, if there has been a regular breakdown of a particular piece of machinery, you can plan to respond to the next breakdown by replacement, having a standby available, etc.

Another way to reduce crises is through contingency planning. Study the key elements of a project (quality, quantity, cost and time for completion), and think through three questions so you will be ready to respond when a crisis occurs:

- What is likely to go wrong?
- When will I know about it?
- What will I do about it?

Some crises are beyond your control. For example, you may have unrealistic deadlines imposed on you; priorities may be changed at the last minute; people will make mistakes; machines will break down; etc. When this happens, take a deep breath, and relax for a few minutes. Think through what needs to be done and consider the alternatives. Then approach the situation in an orderly, methodical way. You don't want to precipitate a second crisis by simply trying to handle the first one.

when things go wrong

1. *Renegotiate.* The simplest action when you can't meet a deadline is to renegotiate the due date. Perhaps there is enough flexibility that a day or two longer doesn't really matter.
2. *Recover lost time during later steps.* If, in the early stages of a project, a step takes longer than planned, re-examine time allocations for the remaining steps. Perhaps other time can be saved so that overall time on the project will not increase.
3. *Narrow the scope of the project.* Once the project is under way you may find it will take longer than anticipated to accomplish everything you planned. When time is critical, you may have to eliminate some non-essential things to meet the deadline.

4. *Deploy more resources.* You may need to put more people or machines on to the project. This option clearly increases the cost so it represents a decision choice of weighing the cost against the importance of the deadline.
5. *Accept substitutions.* When a needed item is not available, you may be able to substitute a comparable item to meet your deadline.
6. *Seek alternative sources.* When a supplier you are depending upon cannot deliver within your time frame, look for other suppliers who can. (You may choose to pursue other sources before accepting substitutions.)
7. *Accept partial delivery.* Sometimes a supplier cannot deliver an entire order but can deliver the amount you need to get you past a critical point. After that, the remainder of the order can be delivered to everyone's satisfaction.
8. *Offer incentives.* This option calls for going beyond the terms of an agreement to get someone you are dependent upon to put forth extra effort. It might be a bonus clause in a contract for on-time delivery, or a penalty clause for late delivery, or simply buying someone lunch to put forth an extra effort.
9. *Demand compliance.* Sometimes it is necessary to stand up for your rights and demand delivery according to the agreement. Occasionally, an appeal to higher authority will produce the desired results.

15

dealing with your time-wasters

Now that you have read about time-wasters and how to deal with them, take a few minutes to look at your own situation. List as many time-wasters you have experienced as you can. Then select the three most serious and consider ways to deal with them.

List of time-wasters	
Self-generated	**Environmental**

1. From the list of time-wasters select the three most serious. What are they? How much time do they consume? What causes them?

   (i) ______________________________

   ____

   (ii) ______________________________

   ____

   (iii) ______________________________

   ____

2. List possible ways to reduce the impact of these time-wasters.

   ____

   ____

   ____

---

case study 15.1
the programme really works

I have always admired how Bill does so much without seeming rushed. He always seems to have plenty of time when we talk. I know for a fact he rarely takes work home with him. I finally decided to ask Bill the secrets of his time management.

He began by saying he once had a real time-management problem. Because of it, he looked for ways to make better use of time. He read books on the subject and put some of their ideas into practice. Bill explained that the most important lesson he learned was to adapt techniques to his individual situation. He explained the four following basic concepts as keys to his success.

First, and most important, Bill said he always looks ahead. He lists the goals he is working towards, and has a plan to get there. He said he has learned to anticipate when things are due without waiting to be asked. As an example, budgets are due the second quarter every year. Bill does not wait until he receives a memo requesting his budget, rather he works it into his schedule.

Second, he establishes priorities. There is always more to do than the time to complete it. Occasionally this may mean foregoing something he would like to do in favour of something that has to be done. When setting priorities, Bill said he takes into account his management's wishes as well as his judgement.

Third, Bill indicated he learned not to try to do everything himself. He relies on his staff. Bill knows the people he can depend on and lets them do their job. He also trains others until he can rely on them.

Finally, he said, use only those techniques that help you. For example, he said he doesn't make a 'things to do' list most days, because often his days are routine. However, when things begin to pile up, he always make a list and starts at the top.

According to Bill, that's it. Four basic ideas to help get better control over time: (1) know your diary; (2) prioritise demands on your time; (3) use the skills of others; and (4) use techniques that help your unique situation.

1. Do you think Bill's superiors see him as a good manager and why?

____

____

____

____

____

2. How do you think Bill's staff feel about working for him and why?

____

____

____

____

____

3. What do you learn from Bill's approach that could help you?

____

____

____

____

____

five tips for effective time management

1. List and prioritise weekly objectives.
2. Make a daily 'things to do' list and prioritise it.
3. Devote primary attention to your A priorities.
4. Handle each piece of paper only once.
5. Continually ask: 'What is the best use of my time right now?'

office technology to save you time

telephone enhancements

New and improved products are being developed at such a rapid pace that it is difficult to keep up with the latest time-saving innovations. Trends in the industry are in three directions – less costly new models, smaller models that do the same things and models combining functions of two or more machines. Here are a few examples from the ordinary to the exotic that will save you time when properly used.

answering machines

You should consider one for the office, as well as at home. Answering machines allow you to receive calls and return them at your convenience. Newer models display the phone number from which the incoming call originated, so you can decide whether to take the call immediately or have it recorded. There are even portable models you can take with you and plug into the telephone jack in your hotel room. Some of these models double as dictating machines and alarm clocks. Select an answering machine that automatically records the date and time of calls and is accessible from a touch-tone phone for message retrieval.

voice mail

Voice mail ties a telephone system and a computer together for greater capacity and enhanced operating features. You can change the outgoing message, retrieve incoming messages and forward incoming messages from any touch-tone phone. In contrast to answering machine messages, voice mail messages should be complete rather than a request for a return phone call.

dialling features

Some of the latest innovations reduce the time and effort of manual dialling. Many modern telephones have the capacity to store telephone numbers, which can then be dialled by pressing only one or two buttons. The newest feature is voice-activated dialling. Telephones that have this facility can store up to 50 names and numbers and respond to spoken commands. To dial Bill Jones, one simply says 'Bill Jones' into the speaker.

staying in touch

hands-free operation

If you frequently refer to blueprints, maps or papers while talking on the phone, it is much more convenient to have both hands free. Also, with your hands free, you can be doing other things while talking to someone or waiting on hold. Two features allow you this freedom. One is the speaker phone; the other is a headset. The speaker phone is in common use, but you may not have considered a headset. Today they are lightweight and extremely compact. If you make lots of calls a headset will reduce or eliminate sore ears and neck pain.

You can often save time when you are away from your telephone by staying in contact with your workplace. Here are some common ways to stay in touch:

call forwarding

This feature permits you to programme your phone to forward calls automatically to another phone. If you are going to have access to a phone other than the one at your workstation, you can take calls, and callers will never know that you are not at your regular location.

pagers

These little gadgets, which you clip on to your belt, carry in a pocket or handbag or wear on your wrist, have been around for 40 years or so. Today some models will store up to ten numbers for you to call back. Others display brief messages. The most sophisticated systems link to satellites to contact you anywhere in the country.

mobile phones

If you spend a lot of time away from your office, a mobile phone can be both a convenience and a time saver. Today's mobile phones can be used as organisers, minicomputers, videophones and even TVs.

e-mail

This is the most commonly used way of communicating today. You can send and receive e-mails through your computer, digital TV and now mobile phone. E-mails are almost instantaneous and can be used worldwide.

fax transmission

The fax machine transmits written or graphic text over the telephone system and provides immediate delivery of written material. With their ease of operation and inexpensive price, they are in nearly every company and many homes. Many machines can be programmed to transmit during the hours of lowest telephone rates. They will also simultaneously send a message to a list of recipients. Some of the more popular, low-cost machines combine the features of a telephone, an answering machine and a fax machine. Fax boards are now available for your PC that convert PC files to facsimile transmissions.

alternatives to meetings

Meetings can cost a lot of time and money, especially if attendees come from different locations. Occasionally, rather than calling a meeting, consider one of these alternatives:

conference telephone calls

With the assistance of an operator, you can have several people connected to the same telephone conversation. This allows discussion among all participants. Typically, conference calls should be scheduled in advance to ensure reaching everyone.

teleconferencing

Teleconferencing differs from conference telephone calls by tying two or more meetings together rather than tying three or more people together. A typical teleconference set-up has people meeting in a room equipped with voice-activated speakers. Up to 58 national or international locations can be connected. Each location can go off-line to hold a submeeting and then come back on-line to discuss results with others.

videoconferencing

One-way video with two-way audio is the most common form of videoconferencing currently in use because of the high cost of video transmission. However, this could change with new technology. At the present time, you can transmit from a specially equipped conference room or studio, and remote locations can receive video on a standard television monitor. Remote meeting rooms can be equipped for voice communication between them and with the central transmission point.

computer enhancements

Personal computers are as common today as typewriters were 40 years ago. As industry researchers continue to come up with new products, computers are getting smaller, have more features and are more user-friendly. Here are a few of the latest contributions.

portable computers

The personal computer has been reduced in weight to between six and seven pounds. Originally called laptop computers, today's models are called notebooks in recognition of their smaller size. These computers have all the features and capacity of the traditional PC and are available with high-resolution colour screens. The latest models come with a built-in printer. Using the appropriate software, you can keep records of your travel expenses and submit orders by modem or fax. Traditional spreadsheet and word processing software allows you to analyse data and write reports while you travel or attend a class.

modems

A modem connects your computer to others through the telephone system. This allows you to transmit and receive information. By using a service such as Freeserve, you can browse through airline schedules, book your own travel arrangements, including hotel and rental car reservations, communicate with your office, bank on-line and even buy groceries. You can have access to Stock Exchange transactions and handle your own stock market deals. By using electronic bulletin board services, you can exchange information with anyone interested. You can communicate on-line with anyone who has the same service.

scanners

Scanners import printed or graphic material from a page to your computer. There are handheld and tabletop models that work in either black-and-white or colour. These are terrific time savers when you have to edit and update training manuals, policy manuals or procedure guides. They also come in handy when you want to include pictures and graphics in a report or newsletter.

speech recognisers

Automatic Speech Recognition (ASR) uses a microphone for speech input and a microcomputer that processes voice data. Current models have a capacity of several thousand words. These devices take your spoken words and convert them through your word processor to printed words. This eliminates the need to transcribe dictated material from a tape recorder.

electronic notepads

These handheld computers use an electronic pen for entering data. The computer understands printing and symbols the same way other companies understand keyboard and mouse commands. These devices come in handy for taking notes in the field or in meetings.

electronic organisers

Small enough to tuck into a pocket or briefcase, electronic organisers keep track of your schedule and store telephone numbers, addresses and important dates. Many also have a built-in calculator and clock. Some store notes that you type into memory, remind you to do things and provide foreign language translation, a dictionary, a thesaurus and a calendar through to 9999. The latest models will send faxes and have computer games; some even accept handwritten input the same as electronic notepads.

evaluate your use of the latest electronic technology

Tick the items you are currently using and put an X by the ones you want to investigate for possible use:

- ☐ Answering machine
- ☐ Voice mail
- ☐ Voice-activated dialling
- ☐ Automatic dialling
- ☐ Call forwarding
- ☐ Pager
- ☐ Mobile phone
- ☐ Portable phone
- ☐ Conference telephone calls
- ☐ Fax machine
- ☐ Teleconferencing
- ☐ Videoconferencing
- ☐ Portable computer
- ☐ Modem
- ☐ Optical scanner
- ☐ Speech recogniser
- ☐ Electronic notepad
- ☐ Electronic organiser

How do you see the items you are interested in saving you time?

____

____

____

If you are not using the latest technology, what can you do to change the situation?

____

____

____

17

plan you trips carefully

is this trip necessary?

Business travel can consume a great deal of time. Because of this, it presents opportunities to save time by examining current habits and finding better ways. Some of these tips will also be helpful for personal travel.

Before booking your flight, make sure the trip is necessary. Some options to consider are: Can you handle it by mail or telephone? Can the person you plan to visit come to see you? Can someone else go in your place? When you consider these options, you may find you can save time simply by not making the trip.

If you must make the trip, plan the details carefully. Start by writing down your objectives. (What do you hope to accomplish?) Then make an agenda for your meeting that will lead to achieving your objectives. Next, make a specific appointment with the person or people you plan to visit. Follow up with a written confirmation of the appointment and a copy of your agenda. Upon arrival at your destination, reconfirm your appointment by telephone.

If you have several appointments, plan your itinerary to minimise travel distance between them. And be sure to leave enough time to get from one meeting to the next. You can't always depend on finding a taxi or a parking space.

choose the best mode of travel

Although cars are the most common mode of business travel, don't overlook the advantages of travelling by train or air when circumstances permit.

An option often overlooked is to travel by train. You typically arrive in the business centre of a city, eliminating a long car journey, or taxi or airport bus ride into town.

If you have a company travel department or a contract travel agent, you will be expected to make your arrangements through them. Otherwise, you can work through the travel agent of your choice or call airlines and hotels direct. Here are two time-saving tips when booking air travel:

- Try to book a direct, non-stop flight. Not only will your in-flight time be less, but you will reduce the chances of delayed departures.
- Always get information on flights that are earlier and later than your scheduled departure. Then, if your plans change or your flight is delayed or cancelled, you will know what options are available.

If you are moving around in a country, get one hotel group to make all your bookings.

make the most of travel time

The best way to save time at check-in is to bypass the process as much as possible. With hand luggage only, you can avoid queues at the carousel on arrival.

Plan your wardrobe so that you can get by with carry-on luggage only. Since most airlines have a limit of one carry-on item only, take a small portfolio rather than a briefcase and put it inside your cabin case or in a side pocket of your garment bag.

Because of the potential for lost luggage, always carry a minimum of toiletries and personal items with you.

waiting and in-flight time

You can tell the seasoned business travellers. They are the ones who make full use of their time in waiting lounges and on the aircraft. To make best use of your time, take along work that can be handled without reference to bulky files. This can include such things as proof-reading, catching up on correspondence and reading reports, books and magazines.

There is a selection of portable office equipment that will help to save you time. Notebook computers are very popular among business travellers. You can take advantage of a variety of software or just use the computer as a word processor. Also, tape recorders and dictating machines are handy for dictating correspondence, reports, ideas and suggestions that occur to you as you travel.

Listening to your own audiocassettes of business books or other training material can be much more rewarding than listening to airline music or watching a film.

getting to and from the airport

In most cities, you can travel to and from the airport by private car, taxi, bus, train or rented car. In their home city, many people choose to drive their own car, but consider the convenience of parking at both your workplace and the airport. Also, consider the availability of other modes of transport to get you to either your home or workplace when you return. You may find another choice will save you time.

When you arrive at your destination, a chauffeur-driven car is the most convenient option. The driver will be waiting for you, will help with your luggage and will deliver you to your hotel. Taxi service can be convenient also, but there may be a considerable wait at busy airports. Bus services usually involve a delay, as you must wait for the bus to operate to schedule.

All these choices leave you without any transport after you have been dropped at your destination. You must either walk or rely on taxi services for local travel. A rented car can be convenient if your trip calls for much local travel. To save time at the car rental counter, have a confirmed reservation. Most rental companies gather and store in their computer all the information they need. With this information on file and a confirmed reservation, you can bypass the check-in counter and go directly to pick up your car. When you return, use the express check-in system to avoid queuing.

saving time at your hotel

Most of the major hotel chains offer extra services geared to the business traveller. Take advantage of those services plus these other ideas to save time:

- Find the most convenient hotel. Ask the person you are visiting for suggestions. Or have you travel agent check hotels near the address you will be visiting. If several people are flying in for a meeting, consider booking accommodation for everyone at an airport hotel.

- Confirm your reservation with a credit card and get a confirmation reference in writing or make a note of it over the phone.
- Streamline your checkout by asking for your bill the night before departure. Checking your bill the night before helps ensure that everything will be in order.

put your plans in writing

After all arrangements have been made, write up an itinerary of your trip. Include the names of people you will be visiting with their addresses, phone and fax numbers. Include the date and time of each appointment. Show the date and time of departure and arrival along with flight numbers. Also, show the name, address and telephone number of the hotel where you will be staying along with your confirmation reference.

This information should be given to family members, office staff and anyone else who might need to contact you for business or personal reasons. (It will also be helpful to take a copy with you.)

travellers' checklist of timesaving tips

		Yes	No
1.	Is this trip really necessary?	☐	☐
2.	Do you have written objectives and an agenda?	☐	☐
3.	Do you have a confirmed appointment?	☐	☐
4.	Have you chosen the best mode of travel?	☐	☐
5.	Have you booked the most direct flight?	☐	☐
6.	Have you avoided Friday travel?	☐	☐
7.	Have you avoided early morning travel?	☐	☐
8.	Do you have your tickets and boarding pass?	☐	☐
9.	Do you know the flights before and after yours?	☐	☐
10.	Can you carry on all of your luggage?	☐	☐
11.	Have you arranged the best ground transportation?	☐	☐
12.	Have you booked the most convenient hotel?	☐	☐
13.	Do you have sufficient work to stay busy?	☐	☐
14.	Do you have the equipment you may need?	☐	☐
15.	Have you advised everyone of your travel plans?	☐	☐

18

applying what you've learnt

This section contains worksheets that will help you apply time management principles and techniques to your own situation. To complete this section, you need to do the following:

1. *Gather data.* Keep a daily time log for one week similar to the one shown on page 75. This will provide accurate information for you to improve your use of time. Be honest and attentive to detail.
2. *Analyse your use of time.* Working with the data gathered, analyse your current use of time. List opportunities for improvement.
3. *Action plan.* From your analysis, develop specific action plans to bring about the desired improvement in your use of time.
4. *Follow-up.* Six weeks after beginning your time management improvement effort complete the Progress Survey on pages 82–85 to assess your progress, and decide what work still needs to be done.

instructions for keeping a daily time log

- Select a typical week (ie avoid sick leave, personal leave, holiday, etc).
- Record activities at least every half hour. Be specific. For example, identify visitors and record duration and topics of conversation. (Be honest. Only you will have access to this information.)
- Write a comment on each activity. Did something take longer than usual? Why? Were you interrupted?
- At the end of the day note whether this day was typical, busier than usual, or less busy than usual. Add up time spent in various major activities (meetings, visitors, telephoning, post, etc), and show totals along with other comments at the bottom of the daily log.

An example is shown on the next page.

time analyser

Use your time log as a basis. Draw conclusions and record your responses to the following questions:

1. Which part of each day was most productive? Which was least productive? Why?

____

____

____

____

____

____

Daily time log	
Day of week: M T W T F S	Date:
Time Activity	Comments
7.00	
7.30	
8.00	
8.30	
9.00	
9.30	
10.00	
10.30	
11.00	
11.30	
12.00	
12.30	
1.00	
1.30	
2.00	
2.30	
3.00	
3.30	
4.00	
4.30	
5.00	
5.30	

Was this day: ______________ Typical? Comments: ______________

______________ Busier? ______________

______________ Less busy? ______________

2. What are the recurring patterns of inefficiency (ie waiting for something, searching for something, interruptions, etc)?

____

____

____

____

____

____

3. What do you do that may not be necessary? (Be liberal since this list is simply for further reference.)

____

____

____

____

____

____

4. What do you do that may be inappropriate? (Again, these are only prospects for further scrutiny.)

____

____

____

____

____

____

5. Where are your opportunities for increased efficiency?

____

____

____

____

____

____

6. On what occasions do you allow enjoyment to override a priority task?

____

____

____

____

____

____

7. Which activities do not contribute to achieving one of your objectives? How can you change this?

____

____

____

____

____

____

8. On average, what percentage of working time are you productive? (Be honest.) What is your reaction to this figure?

____

____

____

____

____

____

planning for improved time utilisation

step 1

State your time improvement objective. Be specific both in terms of how much time you hope to liberate in your weekly schedule and the target date by which you hope to accomplish it.

____

____

____

____

step 2

Identify your areas of opportunity. Be specific. What tasks might be eliminated or reassigned? What time wasters can be eliminated or reduced? What planning needs to be done?

Opportunity	Estimated time saving

step 3

Select those opportunities you plan to pursue. Add up the anticipated time saving and compare it with your target.

Opportunity No 1: ______________________

____

____

Action steps	Target dates

Action steps	Target dates

Opportunity No 2: ____________________

Action steps	Target dates

Opportunity No 3: ______________________________

____

____

Action steps	Target dates

step 4

List others who need to be involved when implementing your changes. This should include review and approval by your managers, as well as the agreement and co-operation of those who may assume part of your duties and/or responsibilities.

Supervisor: ______________________________

____

____

____

____

____

____

Colleagues: ______________________________

____

____

____

____

____

____

Staff: ___________________________________

____

____

____

____

____

____

step 5

Follow up in 30 days. Review your progress and repeat any steps that have not provided the results you anticipated.

Notes ____

____

____

____

____

____

____

____

____

____

____

____

____

progress survey

instructions

Six weeks after beginning your time management improvement effort complete the following survey. It will show where you are doing well, and where you still need to devote attention.

scoring key

Yes – 1; Usually – 2; Sometimes – 3; Rarely – 4; Never or No – 5; Not applicable – NA.

1. Do you have a clearly defined list of written objectives? ______

2. Do you plan and schedule your time on a weekly and daily basis? ______

3. Can you find large blocks of uninterrupted time when you need to? ______

4. Have you reduced or eliminated recurring crises from your job? ______

5. Do you refuse to answer the phone when engaged in important conversations or activities? ______

6. Do you use travel and waiting time productively? ______

7. Do you delegate as much as possible? ______

8. Do you prevent your staff from delegating their tasks and decision-making to you? ______

9. Do you take time each day to think about what you are doing relative to what you are trying to accomplish? ______

10. Have you eliminated any time wasters during the past week? ______

11. Do you feel in control of your time? ______

12. Are your desk and office well organised and free of clutter? ______

13. Have you reduced or eliminated time wasted in meetings? ______

14. Have you conquered your tendency to procrastinate? ______

15. Do you carry out work on the basis of your priorities? ______

16. Do you resist the temptation to get heavily involved in non-productive activities? ______

17. Do you control your schedule so that others do not waste time waiting for you? ______

18. Do you meet your deadlines? ______

19. Can you identify the few critical tasks that account for the majority of your results? ______

20. Are you better organised and accomplishing more than you were six weeks ago? ______

21. Have you been able to reduce the amount of time you spend on routine paperwork? ______

22. Do you effectively control interruptions and drop-in visitors? ______

23. Have you mastered the ability to say 'No' whenever you should? ______

24. Do you stay up to date with your most important reading? ______

25. Did you leave enough time for yourself – recreation, study, community service, family? ______

Total ______

scoring

Add the points assigned to each item. The lower your score, the better. Look particularly at items you rated 4 or 5. These represent challenges for further development.

This survey should be retaken quarterly as old habits have a way of recurring.

19

time management in a nutshell

You need to identify that portion of time over which you have control. Then develop procedures for repetitive operations and/or make use of available technology. You should concentrate on high pay-off activities.

Also, identify and make best use of your personal energy cycle. Use prime time to handle work requiring concentration. If possible, arrange for a quiet period to match your prime time when there are pressing matters.

Next, establish quarterly objectives and construct plans to accomplish them. Maintain some flexibility to respond to unexpected events. Prioritise the action steps required to achieve your objectives.

Analyze your use of time. Keep a time log for a typical week, then examine your activities using the tests of necessity, appropriateness and efficiency. From this examination decide the essential elements of your job and isolate time wasters and deal with them.

Finally, remember that the ideas in this book must be adapted to fit your unique situation. Modify the worksheets if necessary, develop your own personal filing system and use the planning techniques when appropriate. Don't let existing forms and procedures deter you from doing your job.

Keep this programme handy as a reference. To check your progress, make a note to review the book again in three months.